Meghan Markle

A Meghan Markle Biography

Katy Holborn

Table of Contents

I. Introduction: A Cinderella Story for the Internet Age

In 2017, American cable television actress Meghan Markle topped Google's annual list of the most searched actors of the year. This would be her second year in a row. She bested, for example, the likes of box office record-breaking *Wonder Woman*, Gal Gadot, and the living legend herself, multiple Academy Award winner Meryl Streep. Compared to these two names, Ms. Markle's acting resume is thin. As a matter of fact, for many people, she seemed to have come out of nowhere.

Only a handful of things can propel a person from relative obscurity to a name in lights. Even little girls all over the world would know the answer to this – a dashing Prince Charming must have found his Cinderella against all odds. They will marry in a beautiful, lavish ceremony before an adoring public and live happily ever after.

Indeed, Meghan Markle's climb to the top of this list and in the minds of the international public is largely credited to her relationship with the United Kingdom's beloved Prince Harry – a romance confirmed on November 2016, and with an engagement announced a year later on November 2017.

That anything relating to Prince Harry is interesting on a global scale comes as no surprise. He is one of the iconic and captivating, late Princess Diana's two sons. The world sympathetically rode along with him and his older brother, Prince William, in the rollercoaster of their parents' tumultuous relationship and ultimately, their mother's tragic death. But the brothers were captivating on their own merits. Prince William had married his own "Cinderella," the much adored Kate Middleton, and they gave birth to beautiful children. Prince Harry, on the other hand, was fascinating for his party boy image and string of romantic entanglements. These modern, young royals were like a breath of fresh air in an old institution, and everything they did was under such scrutiny it was like living under a microscope. When he and Meghan started dating in 2016 and the relationship looked to be very serious, that attention only intensified.

Because their love story isn't just about a mysterious, beautiful, young woman walking into a room and sweeping Prince Charming off his feet. In the Internet Age, the mystery around "Cinderella" can be vanquished with a few strokes of the keyboard.

Search Meghan Markle – as millions over millions of people have in 2016, 2017 and thereafter - and it is immediately clear that this "Cinderella" is a woman with history and complexity. She is her own person – not a blank slate to be transformed by a fairy godmother, not a cinder girl seeking salvation, not a barefoot awaiting fancy shoes to fill.

Minutes or even seconds into one's search, and it is revealed she is older than Prince Harry by a couple of years. A little surprising, but rumors of the prince dating older women was not new. A few more search results and one might discover she is half-black– outrageous to some sad minds in dark corners of the Internet, but she and Prince Harry wouldn't be the first mixed-race royal couple. European aristocracies like the Habsburgs boast of such modern romances, and intriguingly, there is a popular but unproven theory that Queen Charlotte, wife of King George III and grandmother to Queen Victoria, may have been biracial herself.

Search a bit more, and Ms. Markle's largest claim to individual fame is that she was a series regular on the hit American cable show,

Suits. That's all right, one might think. Actresses and royalty have often been linked to the most curious results. Sometimes controversial - as in the case of comic stage actress Nell Gwyn, beloved mistress of King Charles II in the 17th century or Rita Hayworth and Prince Aly Khan in the 1940s; and sometimes to great aplomb - iconic Hollywood beauty Grace Kelly had famously wed Monaco's Prince Ranier in the 1950s. Rumors linking Prince Harry to women in the entertainment industry is also not new, with alleged conquests including TV presenters, actresses, and singers. But the steamy scenes featuring the future royal in black, lacy underwear having a hookup in a legal library in her role as Rachel Zane might give one some pause, just like that fact that Ms. Markle is a divorcee – not unlike the world-shaking and unforgettable Duchess of Windsor, Wallis Simpson, a fellow American who played a major role in the abdication crisis of Edward the VIII in the 1930s. But then again, the Duchess of Cornwall, Camilla Parker Bowles, long-time girlfriend and now-wife of her fiancé's father, Prince Charles, is a divorcee too.

Taken separately, someone who is either of mixed race, an actress or a divorcee seems to have already found a place in a royal family tree. But someone who is all three... well, that is quite new and interesting indeed.

These are just the barest toplines of Meghan Markle's biography– she has not even walked into Prince Charming's sight yet - and there is already so much to know and unpack about this woman, who was suddenly thrust into the international spotlight and inescapably, public scrutiny, in such a short amount of time.

She is such a fascinating public figure, that not only is she among the world's most searched women, she is already the subject of bestselling celebrity biographer Andrew Morton's latest title, *Meghan: A Hollywood Princess*, slated for release in April 2018. Mr. Morton, it may be recalled, is famous for his New York Times bestseller on no less than Prince Harry's own mother, *Diana: Her True Story*.

Early excerpts of Mr. Morton's highly-anticipated biography on the latest princess-to-be are already leaving royal watchers clamoring for more information, and the more salacious the details, the better. He isn't the only one willing to spill the beans too; Meghan's paternal half-sister, Samantha Grant, has been making media rounds and peddling her own upcoming book unforgettably titled, *The Diary of Princess Pushy's Sister*.

People are simply desperate for more Meghan Markle, especially in the days leading up to her May 2018 wedding to Prince Harry. Who is she really, and where did she come from? Is she a social climber and Princess Diana wannabe, as some critics have alleged? Is she really "pushy?" Is she even really "black," as the heated topic of race is unavoidably discussed? What does her extensive humanitarian work and deactivated lifestyle blog, *The Tig*, have to say about her? How did her first marriage, to one Trevor Engelson, fall apart? How did she and Prince Harry fall in love? What will their wedding be like? What kind of a royal will she be, and how will she fit in with one of the toughest and most beloved families in the world?

Put that Google Search quest on hold, and take a break from sifting through page after page of websites and news clippings. Here, we answer these questions and more, as we take a look at the remarkable life - so far - of Ms. Meghan Markle!

II. #BlackPrincess?

Shortly after the announcement of Prince Harry's engagement to American television actress Meghan Markle, the hashtag #BlackPrincess became viral on the social media platforms Twitter and Instagram, as many African Americans shared their delight in the thought of a person of color joining the royal family. The trending hashtag is just one more feather on the digital cap of Ms. Markle, a successful lifestyle blogger even before she became Google's most searched actor. But the label, while catchy, isn't quite accurate.

When Meghan Markle marries the beloved, red-headed royal rascal Harry (formally known as His Royal Highness Prince Henry of

Wales), she will be wife to the man who is in line to the British throne. Prince Harry trails after his father Charles; older brother William; nephew George and niece Charlotte by William and his wife, Duchess Catherine; and other children they might have. According to royal historians, tradition has it that a male royal receives a title upon his wedding. Prince William and wife Catherine Middleton, for example, were bestowed Duke and Duchess of Cambridge upon their marriage. Similarly, Prince Harry is widely expected to be made a Duke and therefore Meghan, a Duchess. Ms. Markle, in short, is not expected to be called "Princess Meghan."

Title protocols, traditions, and expectations aside, her love story with Prince

Harry still refused to shed its fairytale patina, and "#blackprincess" nevertheless became viral, even if it wasn't quite accurate from the "princess" standpoint. The tag's questionable accuracy also stemmed from its more controversial first part, however – that of the actress being "black" to begin with, which has spurred reflection and debate on race and identity in two continents.

Tick a Box / Draw Your Own

The most searched woman on the internet isn't sought on her name alone. The public has shown a marked interest in her ethnicity and many even included the word "black" alongside her name on the search bar. There are plenty of passionate opinion-editorials to find on the subject.

"Reminder: Meghan Markle is Not Black" goes a particularly straightforward article by writer Sandra Rose, citing Ms. Markle's dating history of white men, limited public social interactions with black people beyond her own mother, Doria Ragland, and how observers note that she "doesn't claim us." Cultural commentators, like Elaine Musiwa for *Vogue*, point out that she is half-black or bi-racial, and expounds on how this is different. And elsewhere, such as in a piece by Nicole Adlman for *Hello Giggles*, a simple plea – "Can we stop measuring Meghan Markle's blackness?"

Racial identity and relations are complex in most parts of the globe, especially in the politically-charged atmosphere where this cultural moment - the relationship between a popular, white prince and a person of color – is occurring. It may be recalled for example, that early in the couple's relationship, Prince Harry felt compelled to break his usual silence on his personal life by releasing a statement through his Communications Secretary when 'a line was crossed.' Meghan, a girlfriend at the time, "has been subject to a wave of abuse and harassment" through racially-loaded comment pieces and sexist and racist trolling. Ultimately, he feared for her safety and less than two years later, a serious threat would show just how much he had cause to be – a white powder letter with a racist note sent to her in London in February 2018, was intercepted by authorities. The powder, though ultimately ruled harmless, was initially feared to be anthrax. The incident was investigated by the police as a possible racist hate crime.

Meghan Markle has grappled with racial identity issues for far longer than the public has been pondering it about her (or in some cases, using it against her). In a sensitively penned essay for *Elle* Magazine that has since become one of the most revealing and seminal sources of information about an otherwise private person, she discusses her half-black and half-white parentage and how this has shaped her identity and voice.

Her Caucasian father, Thomas Markle, worked in television as a lighting and photography director. He met her African American mother, Doria Ragland, at a studio in the late-70s. They married, had Meghan, and lived in The Valley in Los Angeles. Meghan shared that their neighborhood lacked in diversity, and how her darker-skinned mother would be mistaken for her, a lighter-skinned baby's, nanny. She had trouble identifying her ethnicity and distinctly remembered leaving the box options blank on a mandatory census asking if she was white, black, Hispanic or Asian. In the acting industry, she was considered "ethnically ambiguous" and found difficulties being cast for a job until she landed the plum role of 'dream girl' Rachel Zane on USA Network's *Suits*.

Ultimately, she would share how she had learned to embrace her mixed-race identity. She 'drew her own box' so to speak, and defined herself - not unlike how her great-great-great grandfather did when the United States abolished slavery in 1865 and former slaves had to choose their own surname.

With her new public role, how Ms. Markle identifies racially may no longer just be about finding herself, however. It isn't just an academic question or intellectual exercise, nor is it just a media talking point or a water cooler topic at the office for the public, either. There could be practical implications. For example, will her inclusion in the royal family affect or re-define British identity, in a highly-charged political atmosphere that has lately "weaponized" race and nationality? Will she, who classifies herself as a humanitarian, use her new position and platform to advocate on racial issues, of which there are several in her new home country? Or will her role as a person of color in a storied institution like the monarchy be largely symbolic? Only time will tell.

Once Upon a Time

Her writing in *Elle* gave the public a glimpse of a sensitive, intelligent and independent woman looking back at a journey and coming out stronger. But like all self-possessed heroines of legend and fairy tale, her story begins with Once Upon a Time.

Born Rachel Meghan Markle on August 4th, 1981, she was raised in Los Angeles, California by her African-American mother Doria, and British-Dutch-Irish-descent father Thomas. Doria is a social worker, jewelry maker, and yoga instructor, while Thomas worked as a lighting and photography director for television for several decades. Meghan is their only child together, and after the couple divorced amicably when she was six years old, she lived with her mother.

Her father, who is a Daytime Emmy-award winner, remained involved in much of her life, however. Meghan would recall to *Esquire* in a 2013 interview that she spent years of her after-school hours on the set of hit 80's sitcom, *Married... with Children* at his place of work. His other credits include working on *General Hospital* for 35 years. This exposure would be instrumental in sparking her own interest in the entertainment industry. Thomas was previously married to Roslyn Loveless, with whom he has two children, Meghan's older half-siblings Thomas Jr. and the now-infamous Samantha Grant.

Thomas Sr., now retired, has been described as a bit reclusive lately, and lives quietly in Rosarito, a beach city in Mexico. Despite his physical distance from his Toronto-based daughter, they are said to speak regularly and Meghan has described him, along with her mother, as being very supportive of her. After the engagement announcement, he and Doria released a joint statement through Clarence

House, sharing their joy and good wishes for their daughter and her Prince.

Interestingly, "Cinderella" stories aren't so new to the Markles - what with Thomas Sr. reportedly winning $750,000 in the lottery when Meghan was younger. Part of the sum, according to her half-brother Thomas Jr., went to Meghan's private school education. The future royal attended Hollywood Little Red Schoolhouse, and later, all-girl Catholic institution Immaculate Heart High School in Los Angeles.

Markle, who has been described by her half-brother, Thomas Jr., as someone with "laser focus," is not only the first person in her immediate family to graduate from college, she had done so with a double major. She attended

Northwestern University in Illinois, having graduated in 2003 with a double major in Theater and International Relations. The self-confessed "theater nerd" was active in her sorority, Kappa Kappa Gamma, and had served in the U.S. Embassy in Argentina during her senior year. One of her professors remembered she had displayed an interest in issues of inclusivity, race and women's rights even then, which are aligned with her current advocacies and humanitarian work.

Her sense of social justice cannot be attributed only to her formal education. Meghan credits her parents, and particularly her mother Doria for raising her "to be a global citizen" aware of the "harsh realities" of the world. Mother and daughter are very close. They are frequently photographed together, and the royal-to-be's mom has also joined her daughter to meet with Prince Harry several times. Meghan speaks often, candidly and highly of the youthful, dreadlocked, free-spirited Doria, who even has a nose ring and can still run a marathon. The clinical therapist/yoga instructor / social worker is involved in the geriatric community and at the Didi Hirsch Mental Health Services in California.

Ms. Markle's family life and her past predictably fell into heavy scrutiny after her romance with Prince Harry became public. Everyone has their own secrets and struggles, but being in the public eye can unearth some embarrassing and painful information.

Among the less positive details media outlets have unearthed and reported about them, are Thomas Sr.'s filing for bankruptcy in 2016, Doria's own filing in 2002, and also that of twice-divorced Thomas Jr., who had also faced gun charges that have since been dropped. He reportedly now works as a window fitter in Oregon. Thomas Jr. has been accommodating to the press, and he is not the only family member who is media-friendly – Meghan's former sister-in-law Tracy Dooley had appeared on *Good Morning Britain*, alongside Meghan's nephews Thomas and Tyler Dooley. This is to say nothing of Meghan's estranged sister Samantha Grant, who has been openly critical of her.

Samantha, a former actress, and model herself, hasn't let a 2008 multiple sclerosis diagnosis slow her down from a media blitz; aside from writing *The Diary of Princess Pushy's Sister*, she has been quoted in interviews referring to Meghan as a social climber, and calling Meghan out for not financially supporting their father.

The unconventional set-up and strained relationships is probably why Prince Harry had been quoted as saying his is "the family that I suppose she's never had," a claim that has since been contested by some members of the Markle family.

One would think the royal family Meghan Markle is about to enter shouldn't be too squeamish about tumultuous relationships, as they have well-documented complex histories and entanglements as well as curious characters of their own. But other quarters of the world aren't quite so forgiving. Sometimes, the media in particular can be savage.

"Harry to marry into gangster royalty?" asked *Daily Star*, referring to Meghan Markle's old neighborhood as rough and known for gang wars. A particularly controversial article on the *Daily Mail*, "Harry's Girl is (Almost) Straight Outta Compton," has also been widely panned for sharing the family's bankruptcy woes, alongside racial "dog whistles" criticizing where Doria Ragland and even Meghan's aunt, Ava Burrow, live, describing locales as "run-down" and "gang-afflicted" while sharing crime rates and comparing these environments against Prince Harry's and Meghan's ex-husband,

Trevor Engelson's, fancier neighborhoods. The latter is rumored to be one of the articles that compelled Prince Harry to break from convention and speak out on his personal life, early into their relationship in 2016.

The unprecedented 2016 statement wouldn't be the only time one or both of the royal couple would have to address the racist undertones and outright attacks levied their way. In their first sit-down interview together for the *BBC*, Meghan described the situation as "disheartening," and insisted that she was proud of who she is and where she came from.

Unfair attacks aside, what cannot be doubted is that there are strained family relationships to be found in Meghan Markle's past. But that's not the only skeleton in this closet. A video of 18-year-old Meghan shortly after she graduated from high school, for example, has been circulating the internet. Here, she revealed a strained relationship with her father at the time. While parent-child troubles in the growing up years (Meghan was 36 years old by the time the video came out publicly) can be expected, what is especially jarring is that this video was filmed and unleashed by her former best friend, Ninaki Priddy, a designer in Los Angeles, with whom she had a falling out after an almost lifelong friendship.

Priddy and Markle have known each other since they were two years old and had a close, almost sister-like friendship of thirty years – with intimate photographs to show for it, now also available to the rest of the world thanks to Priddy (and of course, the tabloid industry). Among the photos shared were of the best friends as children, at proms and dances, in school at the Little Red School House and Immaculate Heart High, on road trips and vacations (including one in front of Buckingham Palace!), and at Markle's beach wedding to first husband Trevor Engelson in Jamaica in 2011 – where Priddy had been her maid-of-honor. The bond between the two women ceased shortly after Meghan's divorce, for reasons Priddy has not specifically disclosed outside of saying certain revelations after she met with Engelson ended the friendship. She was no longer in Meghan's life by the time Markle started dating Prince Harry.

III. Meghan Markle: The Working Actress

The Ninaki Priddy video of 18-year-old Meghan Markle was a revelation not only about the royal-to-be's relationship with her father, Thomas, but also about the life and aspirations of a young, aspiring actress. The footage, filmed in 1999, showed the women driving around Los Angeles as Markle prepared for an audition. The role? Dancing in a music video for Latina crossover superstar Shakira, which would have paid her £445 for two days of work. She wouldn't get the part, but as we all know, Meghan Markle's time in the spotlight neither really begins or ends there.

The California girl was exposed to the entertainment industry at a young age, and not just by her geographic proximity to Hollywood. Her father, Thomas, is an award-winning figure in television. Her parents met in a studio, while he worked in lighting and her mother, Doria, was a temp. But the road to Hollywood was not an easy or straightforward one for the actress, who wouldn't find the spotlight until her best-known work as the smart and stunning, legal assistant Rachel Zane in the hit USA Network drama *Suits*.

Before playing Rachel Zane, Meghan's racially ambiguous features made her difficult to cast in a "label-driven" industry, where color was considered an integral part of character. She tried her best to capitalize on that ambiguity by auditioning for pretty much any role, highlighting whichever ones of her mixed features may be demanded of a character. Still, she found herself languishing in a limbo of not being "black enough" or not being "white enough" for clearly defined, black and white roles.

The stunning actress still managed to rack up a considerable resume, however, with credits on both the big screen and the small screen, starting with a small role as "Nurse Jill" in an episode of *General Hospital*. She would log in short appearances in hit shows like crime procedurals *Castle*, *CSI: Miami*, *CSI: New York* and *Without a Trace*; sitcom *'Til Death*; CW's remake of *90210*; sci-fi drama series *Fringe*; sports comedy *The League*; the short-lived, reimagined *Knight Rider* (where she played a cage fighter!), and as a case model for the game show *Deal or No Deal*. She would also appear in a collection of lesser-known TV Series and films, many of which were also made for television.

Her big screen appearances pitted her against some big names in show business, albeit in small roles. She sat between Ashton Kutcher and Kal Penn in an airplane in 2005's *A Lot Like Love*; had appeared as a snarky bartender in the Robert Pattinson (he of iconic *Twilight* fame) movie, *Remember Me*; and made a scene-stealing cameo as a beautiful FedEx delivery girl in *Horrible Bosses* (2011), which starred Jennifer Aniston, Jamie Foxx, Kevin Spacey, Colin Farell, Jason Bateman, Jonathan Sudeikis, Charlie Day and Donald Sutherland.

All in all, her resume reads like that of a quiet, working actor - varied, sometimes random, playing big roles in small projects or small roles in big projects. In interviews, she had talked about her work struggles, and how her parents had helped her make ends meet and pay the bills. She worked a variety of jobs before catching a break, including being a hostess at a restaurant and doing calligraphy. The latter was a part-time job with a memorable and very Hollywood experience; she did calligraphy for the invitations of the wedding between five-time Grammy-nominee Robin Thicke (most famous for the monster hit "Blurred Lines"), and his now ex-wife, film and TV actress, Paula Patton.

It would be her work as Rachel Zane in *Suits* that would turn the tide away from miscellaneous jobs and small roles and propel her into the spotlight.

Suit Up

Suits is a cable TV drama following the work and personal lives of high-powered lawyers in New York City – particularly, that of superstar closer Harvey Specter and his protégé Mike Ross, a legal genius and secret college dropout. At a hiring event faced with a set of unimaginative potential recruits, Mike walks in and steals the show, prompting Specter to take a gamble on him despite his lack of credentials. Specter even keeps Mike's fraud a secret from his storied firm, Pearson Hardman. Though initially hiring Mike for his raw talent, Harvey finds a shared passion for winning and eventually, true friendship with Mike. Together, they navigate the shark-infested waters of high powered New York, internal office politics, and romance.

From the very beginning, Meghan Markle was part of the strong ensemble cast of *Suits*. She played legal assistant and eventual lawyer Rachel Zane, the love interest of the prodigious Mike, from 2011 to 2018. It was a role she could have missed out on. She arrived underdressed for her audition, casually-clad in dark jeans, spaghetti-straps, and heels. To appear more lawyer-like, she popped into an H&M for a $35 little black dress she would later be asked to change into. Another actress, Kim Shaw, was reportedly under consideration for the part as well. Each woman had her own charms. Shaw, a blond, girl-next-door type, would eventually be cast by the same company behind *Suits* in a dramedy for MTV. Meghan Markle ended up clinching the role of Rachel Zane, and her life would never be the same.

Show creator Aaron Korsh credits Markle's sharp smarts and inextricable sweetness for the close. Then-USA Network executive Jeff Wachtel remarked on her urbane edge and chemistry with boyish star Patrick J. Adams, who starred as Mike Ross.

Mike's romance with Rachel is one of the central storylines in *Suits*. She is the straight-laced hard worker and him, the flawed but brilliant rule-breaker. Adams described them as a kind of Romeo and Juliet and indeed, over the course of seven seasons, we watch their sexual tension and love heat up and wane amidst legal drama, office politics, and the weight of Mike's secrets.

Suits is a veritable hit with a viewership of over 1.7 million and is now past the 100-episode mark. It is shown and well-loved in many countries and enjoys generally positive critical reviews, with multiple People's Choice Awards nominations and most notably, a Screen Actors Guild Award nomination for Patrick J. Adams. As of this writing, the show has been renewed for an eighth season – but one that would have to be without Meghan Markle, whose departure was announced following her engagement.

The show's flow is not expected to suffer too greatly. Cable TV executive Jeff Wachtel, who had a hand in casting Markle in *Suits*, remarked that the timing for Rachel Zane's exit was right for a series in its seventh season – a time for change. There may have also been some expectation of these developments anyway, as people on the *Suits* team had to deal with the complications of having a royal's girlfriend on set; increased security measures, call sheet changes for Meghan's schedule amidst rumors of meeting the Queen, etc. What comes as a larger surprise for fans of the show, however, is that it will return in season 8 without Mike Ross himself, SAG-nominated Patrick J. Adams.

A joint exit, just like Romeo and Juliet, after all - but of course, far less dramatically and far less tragically.

IV. Meghan Markle: Humanitarian, Writer, Editor-in-Chief, Etc., Etc., Etc....

In a 2015 essay for *Elle* discussing her identity, Meghan Markle describes herself as, among a "mouthful" of other things, an actress, writer, and Editor-in-Chief of *The Tig*. Prince Harry's wife-to-be is a woman wearing many hats, and bringing Rachel Zane to life on screen is only one of them. She speaks with particular passion about her work as a humanitarian.

In another heartfelt essay, this time for *Elle UK*, the successful actress is very reflective about her fame and how she reconciles it with the hardships she sees in the world, as well as her role in helping to relieve it. She recognizes the importance of the entertainment industry both as a source of escape for those to consume it and also for herself as a working actress with a platform and a chance – as well as a responsibility – to do greater good. "With fame comes opportunity," she writes, "but it also includes responsibility."

Meghan credits how her parents raised her as a source of her sense of responsibility and social consciousness. What she saw growing up, she claimed, was what she became. Her parents were generous, from giving out spare change to sharing meals at hospices and to the homeless. The scope of her own generosity would range from small actions things to huge ones.

As a teenager she spent days volunteering in Skid Row in Los Angeles; as an actress, she volunteered at a soup kitchen and had arranged with series executives for their extra crew meals be donated there. But her advocacies aren't just about material generosity. They are also about knowledge. She decided her website, *The Tig*, should "pepper in what matters," with pieces on social consciousness and self-empowerment, aside from its lifestyle content covering fashion, food, travel, and beauty.

Her sense of activism goes back a long way. In a now well-known anecdote about Meghan Markle, she had once written known feminist voices like Hillary Clinton, Gloria Allred and Linda Ellerbee, protesting the tagline of a dishwashing liquid ad that she had found unfair to women. The commercial would later be changed. She was only 11 years old at the time.

The Tig

Meghan Markle's writing is engaging and charismatic, and while her essays have been featured and read in magazines like *Elle* and *Time*, her playground is the website of her lifestyle brand, *The Tig*, launched in 2014 and shut down in April 2017 after about three years of operation. But because this is the Internet Age, nothing goes away quite completely, even if all that one can see left at thetig.com is a sweet farewell (*"You've made my days brighter... don't forget your worth..."*).

Thanks to tools like The Internet Archive's Wayback Machine (said to archive 445 billion web pages chronicling the evolution of the internet), traces of *The Tig* can still be accessed in the world wide web. These are echoes of the voice and thoughts of the now-ironically more private, but inescapably more public figure behind it. Looking back at a few highlights of the now-defunct website, we get a peek into the mind of Prince Harry's bride-to-be.

Chronicling Moments of Discovery

The Tig draws its name from the shortened mispronunciation of Tignanello, a much-loved red wine with a 600-year history. The "Super-Tuscan" wine comes at a price tag of

$90 to $150 a bottle. It's one of Meghan's favorite things, but that is not the only reason she named her website after it. As the first wine that defined characteristics like "body," "legs" and "structure" for her, "Tig" became a metaphor for "getting it" – an ah-ha! moment of discovery. And so her website became a depository of enlightening moments in travel, food, fashion, beauty and other experiences, whether drink-related or not. The ideas, tips, and advice she shared was about how to get more out of life. Some cultural commentators have likened it to Gwyneth Paltrow's *Goop* (running since 2008), and Blake Lively's *Preserve* (launched in 2014 and shut down in 2015).

Food and Wine

Given its namesake, there is no surprise that *The Tig* had a good collection of entries on food and wine. Among them are recipes for both homey dishes and slightly unconventional ones. She shared how-to's for mushroom pasta with creamy truffle sauce, smoked salmon dill dip, beet cheesecake, sweet potato and white bean soup, and, "Combining two of every lady's classic loves," red wine hot chocolate – just to name a few. She also confessed to a love for hot sauce in her food.

Books, Movies, and Music

Cultural commentators have observed that *The Tig* hints of a fairly grounded celebrity.

She showed a liking for cozy, low-key affairs, including morning snuggles with her rescue dogs and intimate affairs with her friends. Like many bloggers, she also had a listing of her beloved books, movies, and music. She used to share her favorite playlists, and her taste in music has been described as eclectic. Among the artists mentioned were Christine And The Queens, Sophie Ellis-Bextor, and Steely Dan.

As for books, she once shared a listing of targeted vacation reads, which included Michael Ondaatje's *The English Patient*, a love affair set in World War II.

Politics

Ms. Markle's *The Tig* wasn't afraid of getting personal, while also looking at the big picture. The actress did not shy away from discussions of race and had even shared her family's experiences. In 2015, a piece called "Champions of Change" honored change-makers like Martin Luther King Jr., Harvey Milk, Gloria Steinem, and, among these iconic names, she also thanked her own parents. Another post, "Because You Must," discussed the imperative for women to vote, along with a history of how the right to do so required the shedding of "blood, sweat, and tears."

Health and Beauty

The Tig also became an outlet for Meghan to share her healthy lifestyle and beauty regimen, from her passion for yoga to her favorite facialists all over the world. And how wouldn't she know about something so specific in various corners of our globe? Her wanderlust and travel chops are also well documented on *The Tig*.

Travel

Ms. Markle used her website to share her travel experiences, notably one of a month-long, *Eat, Pray, Love*-type of excursion in Italy. The *Tig* also featured an impressive collection of insider travel advice on locales from all corners of the world. She and her gaggle of international connections provided comprehensive guides on cities as varied as Athens, Bali, Bordeaux, Madrid, New York, and Paris.

Famous Friends

Meghan's life as it can be glimpsed in *The Tig* isn't just about having fine things, but also being surrounded by fine relationships. She speaks often and highly of her mother and of hosting her friends. She is also a lover of dogs, specifically her rescue dogs Bogart (a Labrador-Shepherd cross); and Guy (a beagle). Both are now – naturally! – almost as famous as she. Because of her celebrity status, however, it is unavoidable that Ms. Markle's writing peppered with mentions and contributions of impressive friends and acquaintances.

Elettra Wiedermann, daughter of Isabella Rossellini, curated a travel guide for one of Meghan's beloved cities, Paris. Canadian crooner and international superstar Michael Buble had contributed too, with his favorite tracks for the Christmas season. Markle became fast friends with sporting legend and icon, Serena Williams, in 2016, and their friendship is mentioned in the blog.

Life Advice

On the whole, *The Tig* was about a life well-lived, from material, quantifiable things to less measurable things like extraordinary experiences and even improving your outlook. She had entries on improving positivity, and advice on self-love and fostering independence. Among her most interesting tips? Going to movies alone and treating oneself out to dinner!

From Refugee Camps to Red Carpets

The Tig has been shut down since April 2017, and Meghan Markle's social media accounts would follow not long afterward in early 2018, in keeping with her status as a future member of the British royal family. This is not unexpected because, though some members of the monarchy do have official accounts, these are maintained by their respective households and are comparatively impersonal in terms of content. Kensington Palace's communications team are expected to post for her after their wedding – as is the case for Prince William and his wife, Duchess Catherine.

It's a lot of platform to lose; at the end of 2017, Meghan's Instagram following clocked in at almost 2 million, while her Twitter account has crossed the 350,000 mark. But with the deactivation of *The Tig* and her other social media presence, Ms. Markle could hardly be described as silenced.

Her voice has only been getting bolder and louder over time, as she championed a multitude of causes. She is an advocate for UN Women, and her work there has brought her into the sphere of both women in power, and those who need their voices heard.

In Kigali, Rwanda, for example, she met with both female parliamentarians and grass-roots leaders at a refugee camp. As an advocate for the organization, she has also graced the stage for a powerful speech on International Women's Day, courting a standing ovation from UN Secretary-General Ban Ki-moon himself – one of her heroes. He, along with politicians and diplomats like Madeline Albright, are the kind of people she looks up to and considers as celebrities.

Meghan Markle would be making her way to Rwanda several times. Aside from going there for UN Women, she also stopped over in her work as a global ambassador for World Vision, looking at projects in providing access to clean water. Her tasks for World Vision also included travel to Delhi and Mumbai in India, to advocate for menstrual health. She would write about her experience in *Time* Magazine, linking access to feminine products as a contributing factor in women's potential.

Meghan Markle has also been active as a Counsellor with One Young World, an organization that brings together young leaders from all over the world. In this role, she has shared the stage with the likes of Canada's media savvy Prime Minister, Justin Trudeau.

Anyone can get whiplash, having to navigate the extremes of having so much in her life as a successful television actress, and the lack of basic necessities she sees in her charitable works. She had described the dissonance as a swinging pendulum. But from what she has shown the world, she is able to navigate Hollywood and humanitarianism with aplomb. As she had mentioned on her website, she shifts between refugee camps and red carpets.

Now, she adds another "R-" a new responsibility, a new cap to wear, and another side to her already multi-faceted life – Royalty.

V. When Harry Met Meghan

Here's another twist on how this modern-day Cinderella story is not like the well-worn fairytales of old. A short search can demystify the titular queen of all mystery girls, yes, but let it not be forgotten that in Meghan and Harry's tale, "Prince Charming" has his own interesting backstory. To begin with, he has a name. *The* name - Windsor.

And what a complex history it carries.

Diana's Son

His Royal Highness Prince Henry of Wales was born in London, England on the 15th of September, 1984. He is the second son to Charles, Prince of Wales, and Princess Diana, formerly Lady Diana Spencer, daughter of Earl Spencer. There is no discussion of Prince Harry without an understanding of his complex upbringing.

The blond and blue-eyed Diana was a stunningly beautiful English rose, but she wouldn't leave a legacy of being "The People's Princess" based on these legendary looks alone. She had already moved in the circles of the royal family since childhood, but she wouldn't be catapulted into the limelight until her courtship and eventual marriage to the reserved heir to the British throne, Prince Charles, who was 13 years older.

They married on the 29th of July, 1981, in a ceremony broadcast the world over that would eventually be dubbed, "Wedding of the Century." Prince Charles and Princess Diana would have two sons – William Arthur Philip Louis, born in 1982; and "Harry" himself, Henry Charles Albert David in 1984.

Prince Harry's parents, unfortunately, would not have a happily-ever-after together. Their years of marriage would be known for difficulties, including issues of infidelity as well as Princess Diana's depression and bulimia. The couple's separation was announced in 1992, and their divorce was finalized in 1996. Charles would eventually go on to marry longtime, on-and-off flame and controversial figure, Camilla

Parker Bowles, in 2005. Diana's life after her royal marriage, on the other hand, took a tragic turn much earlier on. She died in a 1997 car crash while evading intrusive paparazzi in Paris. Also dead were her boyfriend, Egyptian film producer, Dodi Fayed, and their driver.

The world was shocked by Diana's sudden death. She remained a public figure and was beloved all over the world for her beauty and humanitarian work even after she and Prince Charles divorced. During her lifetime, she was associated with at least 100 charities. The world mourned her loss, and felt special sympathy for her two handsome sons, William and Harry (then aged 15 and 12 years respectively), especially when they bravely joined their mother's funeral procession.

Millions of people tuned into the funeral ceremony and procession, just as they did during the events of Diana's life as a royal, just as they did for her wedding to Prince Charles.

The same blinding glare of the spotlights and camera flashes would follow her sons and those they loved for the rest of their own lives.

The Bad Boy Party Prince

All young people make mistakes as they grow older, but for someone like Prince Harry who's got the eye of the world on his every move, these mistakes can make it to the front of tabloids all over the world. There are many reasons why Prince Harry has been called "iconoclastic" and "royal rogue" in the press, among them:

Admitting to underage drinking and smoking marijuana in 2002; getting into a scuffle with paparazzi outside a London club in 2004; being accused of cheating at the storied Eton, an all-boys boarding school; wearing a Nazi-themed outfit to a "Colonial and Native" costume party in 2005; using a racially insensitive term on a fellow soldier who was of Pakistani-descent in 2006; accused of animal cruelty in 2010 during a polo match; and unforgettably, getting photographed naked in 2012, after a game of strip billiards in Las Vegas.

What would follow these misadventures are spectacular spreads on tabloids and other media, and cycles of criticism, staid official statements and public apologies, before the next misstep – and all the above incidents is to say nothing of the string of women linked to the Prince during his time as one of the world's most eligible bachelors.

Still, it wasn't all fun and games for Prince Harry. Like his late mother and his father, Prince Charles, he was heavily involved in charity work and had other, very serious pursuits. In May 2005, he enrolled at Sandhurst and would eventually join the Household Cavalry. He served in Afghanistan in 2008. Afterward, he trained as a helicopter pilot with the Army Air Corps and did a second tour of duty in Afghanistan in 2012.

After ten years of service with the British Army, he ended his military career in 2015 to focus on charity work and his duties as a Prince, but the military was never far from his mind or heart – being a champion for the cause of wounded soldiers is one of his most prominent and cherished roles. Indeed, his and Ms. Meghan Markle's public debut as a couple was in Toronto in 2017, at the Invictus Games – an international sporting contest for injured, wounded and sick, serving or veteran servicemen and women – that he launched in 2014.

Everyone loves the image of a reformed rake, but the truth is, Prince Harry has been heavily involved in many works of charity for a long time now. He set up Sentebale in Africa with Prince Seeiso all the way back in 2006, in honor of their mothers. The charity focuses on the needs of children from Botswana and Lesotho, who are in extreme poverty and affected by HIV/AIDS. Princess Diana, it may be recalled, was one of the most influential advocates for those suffering from the disease in the 1980s- a time when so much misinformation, fear, and shame was attached to it. Prince Harry would continue this legacy by working with the Terrence Higgins Trust. The very modern and tech-savvy royal would also take an HIV test live on social media platform Facebook, to normalize HIV testing and to show that it can be easy to do. He would also take a public test in Barbados with superstar Rihanna on World AIDS Day

2016. Prince Harry is also a patron of WellChild, a charity for sick kids, and had recently founded the Heads Together campaign alongside the Duke and Duchess of Cambridge. Heads Together aims to foster better, more open discussions on mental health, as well as raise funds for mental health services. It may be recalled that Prince Harry's mother, Princess Diana, had publicly admitted to mental health issues during an interview with journalist Martin Bashir in 1995.

Prince Harry paints a picture of a global citizen with social consciousness, even from his position of privilege and fame. In this sense, it seems almost destined that he would meet and fall in love with someone like actress and humanitarian, Meghan Markle.

The Road to You

But before there was Meghan, the world's most eligible royal had romantic entanglements aplenty – both rumored and real.

In 2003, Prince Harry was linked to TV presenter Natalie Pinkham, who has since married and had two children. Shortly afterward, in 2004, he met model Cassie Sumner at a London nightclub. It would reportedly be the last of their scandalous encounters. This short meeting would leave a lasting impression though, thanks to a racy account shared by Ms.

Sumner, which included details on touching and flirting.

Zimbabwean national, Chelsy Davy, would capture the Prince's attention for a far lengthier period of time - much longer than even his relationship with Meghan Markle before he eventually proposed to her. Prince Harry and Ms. Davy became an item during the gap year he spent in Africa, and they dated on and off from 2004 to 2011. He had even brought her to his brother's wedding in 2011. Though the romance didn't bring them down the aisle, it has since been revealed that they remained friendly.

Prince Harry had shorter rumored romances in these unsteady relationship years – with hit show *X-Factor* host Caroline Flack; and

Norwegian singer Camila Romestrand. The entertainment industry continued to prove a romantic lure for the redheaded royal indeed, as his latter love interests were also in the fields of fashion, movies, television, and music. He was linked to posh actress/model Florence Brudenell-Bruce in 2011, now married to multi-millionaire Henry St. George. He reportedly dated another well-heeled actress, fellow aristocrat Cressida Bonas (said to have been introduced to him by his cousin Princess Eugenie), from 2012 to 2014; Mollie King of girl group The Saturdays was a brief interest in 2012; and he had reportedly cozied up to pop star Ellie Goulding in 2016. He has been acquainted with the singer for years now – she performed at his brother's wedding in 2011 and for the Invictus Games in 2014.

Prince Harry's eventual Cinderella, Meghan Markle, has a considerable, rumored and real romantic history herself. Canadian chef Cory Vitiello, a lifestyle TV figure and successful restaurateur, was in the picture from 2014 to 2016. She was briefly linked to golfing superstar Rory McIlroy before that, though there was never any confirmation of a relationship between the two. The most notable of her past romances was with American film producer Trevor Engelson, whom she was with from 2004 to 2013. Engelson's film credits include *Remember me*, *License to Wed*, *All About Steve*, and a few television projects, including *Snowfall* and a *Heathers* remake.

While Meghan's dating past presents a much shorter list than Prince Harry's, it is her deep and lengthy romance with Engelson that had her critics' eyebrows rising. They met when she was just a little over a year out of college on a night out in Los Angeles, and the pair were together for around seven years, engaged in 2010 and married in 2011. The marriage ended in a no-fault divorce in 2013, for irreconcilable differences.

Speculations abound on the reasons for the collapse of the marriage, with rumors swirling left and right from both named and unnamed sources. Some have claimed the end came out of nowhere, while others say fame may have changed Meghan after several successful seasons of *Suits*. Other say the long-distance relationship – she was based in Canada for the television show she starred in, while he ran an office in Los Angeles – was a contributing factor. The parties themselves remain mum on the subject.

A Whirlwind Romance

Prince Harry dates an actress… it could have been any headline on any paper about most of the beautiful women abovementioned since the public took interest in the royal's personal life in his late-teenage years. But in July 2016, he was set up on a blind date with *Suits* actress Meghan Markle and neither of their lives would ever be the same.

The Prince and Meghan were set up by a female mutual friend, whose identity they kept secret to honor her privacy. Though this theory is yet to be confirmed, some royal watchers and amateur sleuths speculate the friend might have been fashion designer Misha Nonoo. She straddles the lines between fashion, entertainment, and royalty on two continents. She was previously in a romance with Alexander Gilkes, a friend to the Princes William and Harry, and also enjoys connections with Princess Eugenie on top of having the skills and networks to be able to dress stylish stars like Emma Watson, Cate Blanchett, and Meghan Markle. Interestingly, Meghan would wear a white, button-down Misha Nonoo shirt called

'Husband' to her and Harry's public debut as a couple at the Invictus Games in 2017.

Another possibility is one Violet von Westenholz, who has long moved in royal circles and also became friendly with Markle while working in P.R. for Ralph Lauren. No further information is forthcoming from the royal couple or any of the "accused," however, and the identity of their matchmaker is still a mystery.

Regardless of who may have set up the royal couple, sparks flew right away. In a candid interview with the BBC, Prince Harry described himself as "beautifully surprised" when he saw her and that he knew he had to 'up his game.' He must have been on point, as he and Markle would go on two consecutive dates in London. A few weeks after that, in August, they went on a five-day vacation in Botswana, a quiet country in southern Africa boasting a low population density and a lot of protected land devoted to the wilderness. There, they really got to know each other; they had limited direct knowledge of the other person prior to dating, even though they were both in the public eye. Prince Harry had not seen *Suits* nor heard of Meghan Markle before, while she did not grow up in the tabloid culture that has hounded him and his family. Thus, while holidaying together in Botswana, their love blossomed under a blanket of stars, in the middle of the relatively untamed wilderness.

It is a country and continent close to the Prince's heart; it was a place of refuge after his mother's untimely death, and ever since then has become a place where he can relax and be himself. He has returned repeatedly for his charities and wildlife conservation work, as well as - if some sources are to be believed – romancing several other women prior to Ms. Markle. After all, who wouldn't be impressed by stunning views and magnificent wildlife in the ultimate glamping date?

Their quiet romance wouldn't remain so for long. The irrepressible tabloids were quick to catch on a good story, and by October of that year, reports were already circulating on the couple's relationship. Prince Harry and Meghan Markle stayed mum on the subject until an unprecedented November 2016 statement from Kensington Palace on behalf of the Prince was released. In it, the romance was confirmed amid condemnation of how Ms. Markle had been represented by some media outlets, and how was being harassed by trolls. The statement referred to Meghan as the Prince's girlfriend – a distinction that would be even clearer come December of that same year when photographs finally emerged of the elusive couple. Papers published photos of the Prince and Ms. Markle out and about in London.

The New Year brought even more romantic milestones. Reports circulated of Meghan meeting Harry's sister-in-law, the Duchess of Cambridge in January 2017, and in March, they attended a friend's wedding in Jamaica. *The Tig*, Meghan's lifestyle brand and website, says farewell shortly afterward, in April. In the following month, she attended the wedding reception of the Duchess of Cambridge's sister, Pippa Middleton, as Prince Harry's date. May 2017 may have also been the month that the Prince sought his grandmother, the Queen Elizabeth's permission to marry Meghan.

The couple returned to Africa and August, stirring up a fury of engagement rumors. But no announcement was made soon after, even with an eventful September – Markle appeared on the cover of *Vanity Fair* proclaiming their love, and they appeared together officially at the Invictus Games held in Toronto.

November of 2017 was monumental too – The month saw Meghan leaving her hit show and moving to Kensington Palace. They announced their engagement on the 27th and held a photo shoot at the Sunken Gardens of Kensington Palace. On the 28th, it was announced that the marriage was set for May 2018, at St. George's Chapel, Windsor Castle, and that the Royals would be footing the bill.

VI. Another "Wedding of the Century"

As of this writing, the upcoming wedding between Prince Harry is still a month away but royal fever is already in high gear, with details on the big day emerging little by little. One thing's for sure though – it would be a relief for anyone that it's a royal family paying for this extravaganza!

The Proposal and That Ring!

The wedding is sure to be a spectacle for the millions expected to witness it on television screens all over the world. In high contrast, the low-key couple were engaged quietly at Kensington Palace during a cozy evening while preparing a meal. They would recall the sweet proposal during an interview with the BBC, sharing how the Prince romantically got down on one knee and how "she didn't even let me finish."

The stunning ring placed on her finger by the Prince is said to have been designed by Harry himself. It features a center stone from Botswana in memory of their magical time there together, flanked by two side stones from Princess Diana's collection – a sweet gesture in honor of the beloved mother who remained a constant influence in the Prince's life. The stones rest on a yellow gold band.

Meghan's upcoming wedding band is expected to carry some history too; by royal tradition, Welsh mines have been the source of gold for royal wedding bands since 1923, when the Queen's parents, King George VI and Elizabeth Bowes-Lyon, married. It would be the same for the Queen and Prince Philip in 1947, and for Prince William and Kate Middleton in 2011.

The Wedding Dress

Meghan Markle's lifestyle brand *The Tig* chronicled the eye-opening discoveries of a well-lived life. This beautiful woman is a connoisseur and a tastemaker, and many are eager to find out how her sense of style will translate to a wedding fit for a royal – especially when it comes to *the* dress.

Photos of Meghan Markle in a wedding dress are easy to find. In character as Rachel Zane for her hit show *Suits*, she was beautiful in a deep V-neck, A-line gown by Anne Barge. Images are also available from her first marriage to Trevor Engelson in 2011. They held festivities before 100 guests in Jamaica, with a traditional Jewish chair dance and beach games and barbecues. The bride was outfitted in a bohemian-style, strapless sheath dress adorned with a jeweled belt. It was very boho chic and indeed, she would later share a taste for simple styles and subtlety, counting Carolyn Bessette Kennedy's iconic Narciso Rodriguez dress as among her favorites.

For her wedding to Prince Harry, royal watchers are expecting a departure from the beach look and hoping for Couture and tasteful style risks – which she had displayed a flair for in her official engagement photos with Prince Harry, wearing a sheer black, $80,000 stunner by Ralph & Russo. Bets are on for the fashion house that would win the coup of dressing the next royal bride. Names that have been bandied around include Ralph & Russo; Duchess Kate's beloved McQueen; and Meghan Markle's friend Roland Mouret. This is expected to be a well-kept secret until we see Ms. Markle garbed for her walk down the aisle.

The Ceremony

The Ceremony will be held at noon, at St. George's Chapel in Windsor Castle. Prince Harry was christened here. It has been reported that The Dean of Windsor, The Rt Reverend David Conner, will be in charge of the service while the Archbishop of Canterbury, Justin Welby, will be the officiant during the wedding vows. He also officiated the recent baptism and confirmation of Meghan Markle into the Church of England, in a ceremony held privately at the Chapel Royal in St. James' Palace.

Their marriage vows will be followed by a romantic and oh-so-royal carriage procession, in a route that was designed to give more people a chance to see the couple and share in their special day.

Not everyone can have a prince for a groom or a carriage procession, but everyone knows a romantic day in celebration of love wouldn't be complete without flowers. The Royals turned to Philippa Craddock for floral arrangements at St. George's Chapel and St. George's Hall. She is expected to work with florists from the Chapel as well as Buckingham Palace, using locally-sourced, seasonal flora like foxgloves, peonies and white garden roses.

The Reception(s!)

Meghan Markle is a lover of food and fine living but either way, dining and especially the wedding cake, is expected to be the very best in any royal wedding.

600 people are expected at the chapel for the ceremony and the luncheon reception at Windsor Castle, hosted by the groom's grandmother, Queen Elizabeth. A private sit-down dinner for 200 will later be held at Frogmore House, this one to be hosted by Prince Harry's father, Charles.

To celebrate their love this season of Spring, the Royals turned to confectioner Claire Ptak of London's Violet Bakery. It has been announced that a season-appropriate wedding cake of lemon and elderflower will be covered in buttercream and styled with fresh blooms.

The Crowds

A royal wedding is always a magical experience, and a show of force from the military always adds that extra oomph. The Ministry of Defense announced participation from various services of the armed forces – The Windsor Castle Guard, Household Cavalry, Navy, Marines, Air Corps, RAF and Royal Ghurka Rifles will be on hand, with music from the Band of the Irish Guards as well as State Trumpeteers. They will be lining the streets of the venue, participating in parades and making music, as if the royals and their guests weren't a spectacle all on their own!

A lucky 2,640 exemplary members of the public will have an intimate view of this historic event – they were welcomed to share the royal wedding experience by giving them access to the grounds of Windsor Castle. What a view!

The Guest List and Invitations

So who are these guests that spectators can look forward to seeing?

There are really still so many unknowns about the wedding, even as it is only just a few weeks away, and the mystery (and controversy!) surrounding the guest list and wedding party are among the biggest ones.

Of Meghan's family, it is not known if anyone has been invited aside from her divorced parents, the very private Thomas Markle Sr., and Meghan's beloved mother Doria Ragland. It is also not known if either or both of them are walking her down the aisle. There have also been no announcements on a Bridesmaid squad, though some of Meghan's famous friends would surely make the wedding even more of a show – she has close relationships with beautiful *Quantico* star Priyanka Chopra, tennis legend Serena Williams, and Canadian stylist Jessica Mulroney. Famous faces from the entertainment industry are expected to be in attendance, especially from Meghan's hit show *Suits* and from Prince Harry's own showbiz connections. Rumors are, a couple of the Prince's ex-girlfriends with whom he remained friends, may also be on the guest list.

The Best Man role is also yet to be confirmed, with speculation falling on Harry's older brother William, or perhaps one of Harry's close friends. Prince William's picture-perfect family is expected to have some participation too, however – he and Duchess Kate's children, Prince George and Prince Charlotte, have already logged some wedding party credentials under their belts, having previously been on their Aunt Pippa Middleton's entourage. Their third sibling, whom the Duchess is due to give birth to in April, is not expected to make an appearance.

There are political and diplomatic considerations to be had, too. The royal couple are good friends with former United States President Barack Obama, and there was early speculation that he and wife, former First Lady Michelle would be invited. That would not be the case, however, and his exclusion from the guest list, as well as that of his successor, President Donald Trump as well as that of the UK's own Prime Minister Theresa May, makes the event seem staunchly apolitical.

As for those lucky enough to get an invitation… it may be recalled that Ms. Markle reportedly supplemented her income when she was a struggling actress with calligraphy, such as what she had done for the wedding invitations of hitmaker Robin Thicke and his (now) ex-wife, actress Paula Patton. Ms. Markle therefore probably has a good eye for elegant writing on a good piece of paper.

The extent of her involvement in the invitations to her own wedding is not known at this time, but the white English cardstock invitations, with elegant gold and black American ink in cursive, is highly formal and steeped in tradition. It features the badge of the Prince of Wales and was made by London-based Barnard & Westwood, the workshop behind royal invites since the mid-1980s.

It would be a dream come true for many a royal watcher to get such an invitation, but in the meantime, as more and more details are revealed on the approach to the special day, most people will just have to wait and see and eventually watch from afar, as one of history's most favorite, reformed royal rogues marries his Cinderella.

VII. Conclusion: Meghan Markle's Second Act

Meghan Markle's relationship to Prince Harry changed everything in her life. Some of these changes started to happen even before they were officially engaged, with only more to come afterward. She had to say goodbye to acting. Passion projects like *The Tig* and platforms on social media that she had spent years of effort to build and nurture had to be shuttered. Immediately following their engagement announcement, she was shuttled to event after event after event, in duties and responsibilities as a royal-to-be.

It can be overwhelming for anyone to be so deeply caught in the public eye. History would tell us this kind of lifestyle can be exhausting and even damaging to even the hardiest of minds and bodies. The initial wave of harassment and abuse that Meghan Markle had to face early in her relationship to the Prince, even just as the latest romantic interest in a long list, was but a glimpse of the kind of scrutiny she would have to deal with. Once she is officially within the royal family, the stakes would only be higher. Inevitably, she will be compared to the widely adored Duchess Kate, Prince William's wife, and the People's Princess herself, Harry's mother, Diana.

Already, some quarters are calling Ms. Markle a Princess Diana wannabe, a kind of "Princess Diana 2.0." But so far, how she will shape her own legacy is still largely unknown.

She isn't a new version of Princess Diana, she is barely even Meghan Markle as she is best recognized – the biracial, divorcee, television actress and lifestyle blogger.

She is at the cusp of a new iteration.

Here, just before her wedding to Prince Harry and the beginning of a new life, we are all at the Intermission. Act One is done; she has quit her day job. She will find a new version of herself that can thrive in the old world of a legendary monarchy, with its enduring structures and rigid rules. Things are about to get bigger and brighter and splashier. We are entering Meghan Markle's Second Act, and what she has in store for the world, we do not yet know.

What we do know, however, is that she is a determined woman with a particular vision for the world she lives in. From her own powerful words in an essay penned for *Elle UK*: fame comes with opportunities and responsibilities, and *"to focus less on glass slippers and more on pushing through glass ceilings."*

Now that's for a modern-day Cinderella!

Made in the USA
San Bernardino, CA
02 February 2019